confusions//delusions

Yelling at the TV feeling so small

Another loved one dead why don't you just take them all

one by one we die

but in support groups we cry we all have pain in life

but no one truly gets it at all I just sit so alone and small

everyone says I can come to them anytime

but it's not their problem they don't wanna here me whine

so I choose to sit and decay don't let anyone see me today I've buried myself in everything that's

bad for my health and I don't want them to be disgusted with me

so let me sit

let me rot

everyone's gonna die so why not me

just let the rest of my family be

please please please!

STOP STOP STOP

take me instead take me instead

if I had a choice she'd be alive and id be dead

Cigarettes

i met a girl she looked so beautiful and when she spoke it was so chemical she said hi my name
is cigarette one kiss of me and you'll love to hate me to death the conversation done she said lets
have some fun and that was about 25 kisses ago

she promised to always love me

she promised to always be there

but now shes taking all my money telling me life's not fair

so now i'm picking her up from a gas station tonight even though i know shell be gone before the
morning light i don't know why i put up with her but i know i cant break up with her we
constantly fight over my choices in life i know i cant win so i just kiss her again further into
despair i go

i make pleads baby why do you do this to me

cancer doesn't sound so pretty

her only rely is we all gotta die might as well die from me

she travels with me everywhere i go i can't help it over this decision i lack control

She promised to love me even when i'm low but i just kissed her for the last time and i need to go
buy more

i know that shes killing me i guess its alright as long as i can afford her ill be just fine because
when my funds are low and without her i'm forced to go i just lose my mind

i hate i hate you so much but i love i love you too much to let you go i've signed away my fate
with you i will stay until into the grave i go

September

Everyone's leaving in September

Welcome to the month of departure

Where everyone leaves you alone

Sitting in your arm chair

January they start to pack

and August is to pack until

SNAP! their gone just like that

No looking back and you're still sitting motionless

As life passes you by

Ballad of the Poets

Poets were put on this earth to suffer because without it where would our thoughts come we thrive under hard times when life leaves you breathing nothing but sulfur but when in serenity we find we finally unwind and calm our troubled minds until the rug is pulled from under our feet down back to the deep we venture writing of sorrow surviving for the serenity to return to our world again

Sin to Win

in order to win you must sin because In modern day society uniqueness is a commodity we give in to peer pressure and change our views more than the weather we call a girl fat because we hate the weight of ourselves we pimp out our bodies like bitches and hoes looking for love and purpose in fashion and the club existing without any real thoughts and more then enough self doubt that never goes away no matter how many bottles you drink to drown we bully the kid that can't afford Nike and anything in your playlists tells you to sell dope and buy jewelry I am not here to be anti drugs or to say not have nice things but what if there warning you that you don't want that because if you live by the gun one day a gun gets pointed at you you don't have to sin to win don't let peer pressure break you even if they're your closest friends we are all created equal and no matter what we have no squeals so make you life yours because when we fall into the grave the peer pressure is gone and you're left with an eternity to reflect the life you lived

God Bless

God bless america land of the free

God bless america where we take away your rights and give you an STD

God bless america where it's citizens hate their homeland

God bless america the country that takes the world and tries to play dad

God bless america where sin is welcomed in

America there is no god bless because you're doing away with him

decision

It was the abortion or new tattoo

so I smiled when I said this is what I want when I gave the artist a picture of you

Worth

A psychedelic life with the love of an amazing woman is the only one worth living

the final love letter

Dear child I will never know

It breaks my heart to let you go

me and your mother aren't together this I know

And we wish we could take care of you so with tears in my eyes

I must confront that we'll never meet face to face

and as I cry now I shall forever because you are my pride and joy

not a surgeons test toy I love you and I always will me and your mother

but life is hard sometimes I just wish we'd met Instead of paying for your death...

love, Mom and Dad

Goodnight Mary Jane

Lay me down to rest the bullet holes like goodnight kisses fill my chest
is this a dream or a reality because I am too blind to see please answer me my heart beat starts to
fail is there anymore will power left in me? was the hell you dragged me through that consuming
is it my spirit and soul I surrendered to the wind when I picked a fight with the demons I have
locked within or was it the drugs I stole to fill my emptiness not to worry the angry dealer found
me with a 12 gauge and he didn't miss so as the bullets exit my body I see the image of an old
math teacher saying

class dismissed

Cheshire cat

I hate my reflection for when I see the dark circles under my eyes from the rest thoughts of you have stolen from me at night or the hollow face I wear sometimes comes a plastic smile when others see me but alone I wear the nothingness I feel inside and I lie to myself and say i'll get over you in due time so now I sit back against the wall I recollect all of our memories together and it only makes me feel small like a vanishing act vanishing like a *Cheshire Cat*

As I Sleep

I dreamed of an abyss searing red scaring my flesh and choruses of screams like mine individually they tell of the wicked lives they lived together they tell a story of how we were damned from the start i try not to scream i try to remain silent and unnoticed by the endless dismal barren pit the red now revealed to be flames increase and screams of pain agony and sorrow flood out uncontrollably tears evaporate as soon as they leave my eyes where am i what is this abyss is it my final resting place i hear a scream unlike all the rest not one of pain or self reflection but of shear pleasure i am in flames but my body goes ice cold i am in pain but can no longer scream what is this abyss from my mind it will not dismiss

Midnight my friend

Hello midnight we meet again my distasteful friend my lack of sleep is killing me but the contents of my mind bring together our embrace every night this pattern holds no end in sight so I sit here writing criticizing myself in a way no one else can or wants to be criticized themselves I rip my mental apart with each passing thought praying that I wasn't put on this earth to rot my eyes are bloodshot and the positive serenity that I crave and want back with me will not let me keep it's presences but midnight is always a comfort to me it tells me of an assured bad morning and another emotionless dazed and confused day

Bastard Son

nothing but a bastard son

obsessed with my own death but the first to run

on a road to self destruction

school is to drool because I never stay awake

and love is to self because it's the only kind that isn't fake

wake is to bake the only times where I don't hate myself

life is a strife where everything feels perfect when nothings alright

death is what comes next because time never has the time to enjoy the light

drugs give the warmest hugs but when they leave make you feel so unloved

alcohol is to diet because how else do I keep this weight off

a blank mind feels so kind

ignorance I wish was mine

only blind men have clean souls

dreams are haunting because they feel real and right until I wake up to the afternoon light

stoned and alone I laugh at everything but feel so alone

Hero

Hero

Hero is dead

Hell dead as dead can be

Uncle Sammy can't help em no more

Cause we shoved him off

This hero ha lost the will to survive

It has been smothered, strangled,shot, and doped up on GREED

Once helpful civilians now plot his demise

Even after his sacrifice

People in suits play games

While others fight the crisis

The hero's power was drained during a political poker game!

HIS PAIN

The rich laughed at

The poor marched

Riots let loose

A few months go by

The hero's in the hospital

Two groups come together to seal his fate

The hero many years ago

Was attacked by a foreign enemy

But now the hero realizes

That the real infection came from within

The hero becomes in debt
While more of his helpful
People in suits help themselves
To money meant for things other then
Cars,whores,alcohol,drugs

The hero becomes
Lazy,weak,obese,envies,hateful
He begins to fall from grace
Faster than ever before
He knows he needs an ace in the hole
In order to survive
Because death is fighting it's way around the corner

Functions

The mind is a funny thing

One minute your suicidal

Next your glad

Then from glad to sad

Then your late to work and start forgetting things

Why is the mind like this?

For I do not know

But then again what if someone

Found out would they want out

Or am I just insane in my motherfucking brain

And that's why I don't understand

how cutting yourself feels good

FUNCTIONS!

Death

When you die do you finally feel at peace?

Or is it just empty?

Do you go straight to heaven or hell?

Or do you just observe life until the rapture well?

Life

Why is it hard to ignore pain

But it's so easy to hate

Are the good things in life free or do they cost us?

Can love always be found

Does suicide show you a way out

Is it wrong to be a basket case

Why are we statistics to the government

Why is murder wrong soldiers do it

Why does every generation have a war to fight

Is money really worth the paper it's wasting

Is life really just a bunch of bullshit

Pure

Society is dead

Civilization is crumbling

But riots remain pure

Love

Your name is a calm

Sweet melody to me

Your smile makes my heartbeat rise

In crescendo

I have new thoughts on love

Is it really weak?

Or did I really just miss the memo

Storm

9:30 at night

couldn't sleep

don't wanna eat

don't wanna even hear a peep

Just want the silence to consume me

To take me away to some place safe

Away from heaven and hell

life and death

alcohol and meth

Don't wanna die

Just wanna live my live

money and fame

it's all the same

it's all piss down the drain

nothing's real

Life is like a Ferris wheel

you turn and turn

But what's the point?

everyone loves

everyone hates

I don't give a shit

so i'll masturbate

Why do you care?

What's in my hair?

Did I blackout on the couch?

People don't care they think I'm weird

I'm preaching to you

Just do what you do always stay true

don't let the storm consume you

Figures

Life is an ocean that's full of peace and happiness

Waiting for us to embrace it

You just have to leave the shore and taste it

No Sleep Required

No sleep required

it's ok I hate sleep

No sleep required

love the lights

No sleep required

bought some nice bags from down the hall

No sleep required

this dope keeps you up all night

No sleep required

come on man COME ON!

No sleep required

because you're dead you overdosed on a bed

Here in America

The city held up by chains

A scape goat casted out in shame

Who knows his pain

Who knows his name

imagine this

imagine that

This man is not a cat

he hears death calling his name

soothing his pain

when he starts to fall

Death grants him a cane

once held only shame

Now only fame

He speaks clear and articulate

He tells the youth numb your pain

Die For Fame

These Days

The tree of life

Was cut down

And used to fuel the fires

of our wicked ways

yes these are dark days

Indeed

Pothead Princess

She is an angel tainted

by the plants of gods green earth

And the liquids of confusion

goes to parties every weekend hell bent

not caring living for here and now

not worried about living forever

Like normal princesses do

Just about a bottle and a plant

but she is living in fear too

fear of being caught by the cops

but this never ruins her moods

she openly partakes in

Her ritual of smoking it and drinking

Until shes numb

Panic

Can't think straight

Can't escape the flood

by hiding behind a crate

I know I'm not good enough for heavens gate

45

45

escape some dead some alive

who cares how who cares why

No love No hate

just the will to create

A new society

A new life

better than before

going against god to settle the score

So they go to war

45

go up and die

none come back

none are alive

satan begins to silently cry

Soul Ball

Come one come all

To the Devils ball

Where he'll condemn you all

So don't be afraid when he opens the gates

Cause deep inside those horrors

Your real dates await

Some sinned unaware but most

Simply had no care

Do you feel that pulling feeling

While you dance

Well little known fact

Escape it you can't

Your soul has been decided for

Satan is here to collect his prize

He is smiling with his diamond blue eyes

Because he will have yours souls in due time

Existance

Suicide bombers blow themselves up everyday

Religious radicals talk about the one way

But i'll sit here with the steady pay of existing

Satan and God are playing cards for me

But i'll just keep my existence with my soul to pay

Cause existing is my way

Airports

Shake me down

Shake me down

no bomb on me

can I go through please?

don't shoot me for putting my hand in my pocket

I just have a phone

no need to call S.W.A.T.

shake me down

Shake me down

nevermind I missed my flight again

My Own Hell

Trapped in a tight space

Unable to move

I fight to get out

With all my might

Here is where I lie

This is the place I've been searching for

For this is where i'll die

stuck in my demise

with no onlookers to sympathize

Eden Ruins

Satan is in the garden

Where he walks everything dies

He leaves behind ashes after his feet

The animals try to run some even try to hide

But in the end everything dies

A smile begins to forms on Satan's

face for only one tree is left standing in Eden

"soon i'll run the place" he proclaims

The Headache

Trapped in the sea

unable to breathe

Desperate I swim

Upwards toward

the dim light I see

I emerge victorious

embraced with my breath

but I celebrate to quickly

for the demon of these waters

has arisen too

Consumer

hungry is the Jackal

Patient is his will

Vile is his soul

Wickedness guides his heart

to the slain ones to consume

their souls

To damn them inside hell

Plea

I hate being alone

Sadness consumes

my soul

I feel like I have no heart just a hole

A gap revealing my pathetic soul

I deserve

No love

No sympathy

Reasons why when i'm alone

I hate myself and sometimes desire to die

Anchor

Being dragged down this anchor is killing me the weight of the water

The weight of my sin it's crushing my body

I can't keep my insides in

This lake of fire surges through my corpse

I, me I'm the gasoline I caused the match to light

When I sinned all out

When I told love to go away

I finally opened my eyes I see the error of my ways

But the fire scorching me from inside out

simply won't go away

Mr.Nuke

Falling toward the ground

Ultimately going to pierce

The ground shattering the awl

Charging forward like a demon out of hell

It has no thoughts only G force

The deadly collision course

uncovering the will of the sender

This awl is a nuke the start of a war

That we the people should have rebuked

Asylum

In a waist jacket of my mind

My captors lock me away for all time

I scream and shout never to breakout

The voices scream and plead for freedom

My ear drums bleed knees weak fearful

Of my transformation my mind has become a whore

Letting any nomad voices through it's door

I can't take it anymore

Doctors said I'm fine

Madness is now

my god, my ruler

Madness has stolen away

My pure innocent mind

everyone sees it even the blind

Trained Monkeys

Do you want it all?

Keep your eye on the ball

Don't talk in the hall

Stay focused

Friends keep you from studying

Work hard play later

But when does later start

Oops didn't get perfect SAT scores

You lost your family's honor

Your a disgrace

A Tale of Two Lives

A poet and a psycho go two by two the poet a man with burning lust the psycho a woman with no such lust the poet screams come be with me! but the psycho has no such care she just cuts her wrist feeling despair the poet screams fuck no please I only bear gifts of love you see the psycho gets in his face and says the man I desire is already dead the poet says so am I...I just killed my wife that stupid hag the psycho pulls out a book those are the souls I have taken the poet laughs and asks why do you kill does it grant you any thrill? The psycho snaps why do you write well before you finish give it a try so they traded and died the poet to hell and the psycho to heaven lust in the poet became a lust for blood and for the psycho begged forgiveness and all in all dust to dust one life for another the poet understood that or at least he used too...

Day Any Night

Too quiet for the day

Too loud at night

I need a spot

In the middle where everything's

Alright

Hell

Fathers dying

Mothers crying

Children fighting

A cause igniting

Everyone's rioting

Soldiers shooting

Guts are spilling

Some are looting

A child born

Prophecy foretold

This child will bring peace

But the missile has other plans

Child is dead

Father survives

Filled with dread

He shoots himself in the head

The product of guerrillas in the mist

Why

Does insanity really mean that you need help?

or is it just a better understanding of life

That the worlds not ready for

So the world gets pissed

Thinking their gonna break the system

So they lock them up and drug them

telling the public that their "helping them"

when really their draining every ounce of creativity

From them crushing their souls killing them from within

But it's a "man's" world so play the rules I just wonder why there so fucked up

Because the good never win and evil has the law to back him up while he screws everyone else

over so I lay in bed and wonder why

Winters Weeping

Sitting in the window

Staring at a dry deserted street

Filled with gas guslers and trash cans

Dead trees are the only life present

All signs of winters tyrant hold tightening

As we reach December

When will we be released

To embrace the warmth of the sun again

Internal Conflict

Rip me

Inside out

Outside in

My soul is making fouls

Breaking out

Can't stand myself

What a hell

Save me bell

I don't want to dwell

In this form anymore

Breaking my core

I'm such a bore

I guess there's a war inside of me

So please set me

FREE

Youth Average

If we've lost ourselves then where do we live inside

Is there really something more

Cause I've lost myself slave to the day

Alcohol won't let me fly

Sometimes we wanna lay down and die

Sometimes we wanna lay down and die

Sitting back with no confidence

Wondering why I can't fly

After class I just get high

high

We were meant to die for so much more

Then these stupid whores

This burns me down to the core

Music and acid make me feel alright

sex well

well it's alright

Drugs?

Drugs damn I need more

www.ingramcontent.com/pod-product-compliance
Lightning Source LLC
Chambersburg PA
CBHW070838290526
45795CB00002B/902

* 9 7 8 1 5 1 1 9 3 5 5 9 3 *